Mirrors and Reflections

A compilation of poetry and prose

Nilupa Rahim

Mirrors and Reflections

YOUNG MINDS PUBLISHING HOUSE

Banrahi (Shiv kumar singh house) Salempur, Deoria, Gorakhpur, Uttar Pradesh, India

Email: - youngmindpublishing1@gmail.com

Instagram: -

https://www.instagram.com/young_minds_publishing

Website: - www.youngmindspublication.in

ISBN: 978-93-91519-16-2

Mirrors and Reflections

DISCLAIMER

The Mirrors and Reflections is a collection of poetry, quotes and microtale.

All the writings published in this book are originally scribbled by the respective mentioned co-authors, the compilers have done best to make them free from errors & plagiarism.

The mentioned characters or events in the book may be living or based on fiction but they neither depict any hate for any people, caste, religion or system nor they are meant to hurt anyone's feelings, against anything.

Publishers would not be responsible, if in case the content is plagiarized, the respective -author will be entirely responsible for misbehavior.

ISBN: 978-93-91519-16-2

Mirrors and Reflections

ACKNOWLEDGEMENT

Firstly, I would like to thank my creator - the most-high for enabling me to appreciate the joy of expressive writing. I am grateful for being able to articulate words in a way that speaks from my heart and brings me comfort and joy as I put pen to paper.

I would like to thank my coach Warren Ryan for his support and encouragement in actualising my dream. If it was not for his continuous, timely push, this book would have remained a dream for years to come.

I would like to extend a special thank you to my dear editor friend for the initial editing process and for plugging my gaps – you are an inspiration to me and I learn from you every day.

To all the amazing people who inspired me to document stories, life lessons and blessings through this medium of creative writing – I wholeheartedly thank you.

Finally, to you, the reader.

Thank you for picking this book up. May it heal, inspire and be a source of support in you being the best version of yourself.

Mirrors and Reflections

About the Author

Nilupa Rahim is a mother, a teacher in adult literacy, mentor, teacher trainer, researcher in linguistics and a bibliophile.

Born and raised in London, England, Nilupa went on to study English Language and achieved her Post Graduate Certificate in Education from the world class University College London - Institute of Education. She has also achieved a first class Masters degree in Linguistics (Teaching English) from London Metropolitan University.

Nilupa draws on her unique experience of life for motivation, inspiration and for driving positive change and impact.

Nilupa has travelled to various places across the world and enjoys discovering new sights and culture. These discoveries satiate her appetite for intrigue but she is most fulfilled through writing poetry and prose and using these for making meaning and processing the world around her.

Her vocation is to serve others, which she achieves through work and poetry. She helps people to align with and live their purpose through self discovery, finding their voice and developing self love and autonomy.

Themes
(explored in the book)

This book is dedicated to Tameem and Naqeeb - my sons, who inspire me every day and who have enabled me to experience immense joy, love and moments of unadulterated bliss in life. I am truly humbled and grateful by these two human beings who are such blessings.

Table of Contents

Foreword

This collection of poems and prose are the work of many years of introspection and reflection written for creative exploration and muse.

The writer draws on valuable life experiences and inspiration to offer the reader bonus lessons (titled life lessons) and reflections to take away long after the book has been read.

This book will leave you touched, awed and inspired to change any thoughts/patterns to a more positive one provoking change and ultimately lead you to focus on...you.

Theme – Love

Between Poetry and Prose

You are poetry,
I am prose.
Together, creating a space
for repose.

You are the ember
that burns bright,
I am the cooling
temper of might.

You are the rush
of energy and fire, (from which)
I doubt I will
cease to tire.

You are the voice of rationale
and reason,
I am a bundle
of heart and emotion.

You are the expressive
with a cool stature,
I am soft and warm
in nature.

Indeed, the bridge
between poetry
and prose,
creates a space for
absolute repose.

Running to you

I come running
Boundless and free.
I come running to you
as me.

I come to you,
Unmasked from the past.
I come uncaged,
from times surpassed.

I come free from shackles,
free from tears,
I seek freedom with you
without the fears.

I want to explore you
free from boundaries
to have and to hold
without any worries.

My Muse

You are my dream,
my existence,
my escapism
and my resistance.

You are my comfort,

My pleasure,
my joy
and my treasure.

You are my strength,
my vice,
my weakness and
my tryst.

You are my fantasy,
my blues,
my mystery
and my muse.

You are my youth,
My maturity,
my prime
and my security.

You are my mirror,
my reflection,
my love
and my satisfaction.

The Light We Are

A shimmering star
you called me.
That I am your light,
that you shine bright because of me -
and the radiance I emit.
Let me tell you however,
that the source of this luminescence
is you.
It may be fair to say that together, we burn bright.
Collectively, we exude light -
transcending into the encounters we have with others.
Together, we burn bright.
Together, we shine.
Shining star -
you
and
I

Steals my Heart

He steals my heart a little more with his words.

He leaves me a little breathless with each interaction.

He steals my attention from all that I do, as I focus solely on him.

Admiring all he is and all he stands for.

Wishing away his trials and tribulations

But feeling emboldened for him and awed by his strength.

I wish time would stand still as I surrender to his husky voice.

Unbeknownst to him, he steals my tears from the sad experiences I have realised, providing me with the comfort that he personifies.

I long to be by his side.

He is my joy,

my pride,

the apple of my eye.

You are...

You are like the soothing balm that

soothes my anguished soul.

You are like the calming wave that tempers my incensed embers.

You are the voice of reason,

that echoes my sometimes muted one.

You are the anchor of

strength and commitment which you see to unwaveringly.

You are the point of articulation, with expressions and inflections

that touch my soul.

You are the smoulder of the eyes

that burn through me with desire.

You are the love that cares, that whispers "I am willing, and here for you".

You are my duas answered.

You are...perfect.

Symbiosis

Those who love; lovers, seldom arrive and meet somewhere. For they are characterised in each other all along.

Manifested through their words,

And exemplified through their words and actions.

The beauty being in their coming together -

In respect,

gratitude,

honour and love.

I see you

I see you in the sun.
I see you in the stars.
I see you in the light of the moon.
I see you in flowers
I see you in trees
I see you in rivers
I see you in the seas.

You are vast.
You are infinite.
You sustain.
I see you through the lens of others.
I see you through mine.
You are serenity.
You are solace.
You are security
You embody the beauty of the world
and my contentment is found in surrendering to you.

Yearning for you

You are the balm that soothes and salves my soul
From the restlessness that I am feeling -
with a strong desire to hear your voice
and a deep yearning that only your presence quells.

I do not recognise myself anymore - for I am not myself.
Who am I?
What is this overwhelming feeling?
Is this love?
Is it lust, infatuation?
Will this feeling last?
Is there longevity?

I don't know the answer and forgive me if I'm wrong - but I feel this much is true.
I feel an undeniable bond between you and me - a special, pure, deep one.
I don't know what this means for us,
I don't know where we'll go.
All I know is that I have given my heart away to yours involuntarily

and I don't want to stop.

I see us living life together,
in sickness and in health.
I see us building a future together, with a much brighter tomorrow.
I see us getting older too...
and what a beautiful sight that is.
I see all this - and more my love.
I don't know how you feel.
I don't want to scare you away,
or make you feel in-burdened.
I realise this may be new for you - it is for me.

Do you feel the restlessness too my dear, the longing and the yearning?
Do you feel the tightly woven tie, that binds your heart to mine?

Gardener

He looked at her,
in awe of her strength -
her gentleness,
her gaily way of life.
He looked at her whilst she was weeding,
pruning and
clearing debris from the overgrowth.

From afar, how he wished together they could cultivate the land,
till and
toil the soil
to create beautiful blossoms
in the garden of their lives.

When I saw you

The first time I saw you,

I fell in love.

A love so precious, so intense, so fierce.

The first time I saw you, I knew my life would never be the same.

You came into the world and became the centre of mine.

The first time I saw and the moment I held you, everything changed. Priorities, perspective, everything in my world shifted.

The first time I saw you, I realised your needs came first; you before me, my child.

That's how it'll always be.

Whisper

I whisper your name

and it resonates in the chirping of the birds, and the budding blossoms.

It echoes in the trees and the rustling of the leaves.

It reverberates through the mountains

and through the waves of the seas.

I whisper your name

and...

nature responds.

Sweet surrender

I see you in the sun.
I see you in the stars.
I see you in the light of the moon.

I see you in the beauty of the world.
I see you through the lens of others.
I see you through mine.

You are vast.
You are infinite.
You sustain.

You are serenity.
You are solace.
You are security
and my contentment is found in surrendering to you.

Unconditional Love

Love is unconditional.
It doesn't care about money
or status.

Love doesn't care about the past.
how you look or don't -
your age, or not.

Love admires,
Love fulfils
Love commits.

Love is being
Love is living
love is freedom.

True love is unconditional.

Edging closer through time

Each passing second brings us a minute closer.

Each passing minute brings us an hour closer

Each passing hour brings us a day closer

and each new day brings me a moment closer to you.

How these periods have passed me by I haven't the faintest but I do know this?

Now that time is edging us closer,

I am waiting in earnest.

Yearning to hear the tinkle in your wonderful voice.

The voice that soothes my soul, the voice that lifts my weary spirits -

that drowns the waves of criticism.

Waiting to look into those twinkly eyes, that speak silently to me of wanton desires and unspent intimacy.

Longing to touch your soft smooth skin and admire that cheeky smile

and just to be...in your sweet company.

Life lesson

Self-love is key. It is a means through which the perception of the world around us is manifested and a lens through which, it is reflected back unto us.

Life lesson

Home comforts such as good, space and privacy provide that external environmental validation to peace and security.

However, being amongst chaos and uncertainty, yet finding that you are still at one with yourself, is what I consider acquiring true peace and serenity.

Home in absolutely where the heart is.

Theme – Companionship

Imprints

Sometimes we meet people who make us doubt everything.

Our practices, character, values and beliefs.

Then there are times when we meet others who make us believe anything is possible.

They fill us with such optimism, joy and love that it is difficult not to see the world through their lenses.

They fill us with such pure conviction that the path less travelled upon does not seem too daunting or treacherous to take.

Especially when they are willing to walk with you partway there.

Indeed, in life, there are times where we meet such people and they have a profound effect, imprinting a piece of their character and a shift is made.

Thereafter, we are never, ever the same.

The Balm

Are you as restless as I?

Do you feel the desire to only hear my voice?

Does your heart seek to speak to mine?

Do you yearn for my presence?

Am I the balm that quells - the one who soothes and salves your soul?

Memorable Moments

I wish you were here,

sharing this moment with me - of nature walks, and trails, and of the birds and the trees.

Of gardens, of rivers, and of the bays and the seas.

I wish you were here,

sharing this moment with me - of faraway tours of lands unseen,

of new sights and smells and of

lush, lush green.

I wish you were here,

sharing this moment with me - of breaking dawns and hazy noons,

of tranquil twilights across the dunes.

I wish you were here,

sharing this moment with me -

of moonbeam, meteorites, and stars that shine bright,

a perfect scene

as we admire the sight.

Travel Companion

Hold my hand, my dear

and don't let go.

Guide me through the trials of life -

when I am lost, and unforeseen events unfold.

Hold my hand, my dear

and don't let go.

Envelope me in your steely resolute,

holding firm when the surround is fractured.

Hold my hand, my dear

and don't let go.

Show me the path less traversed, clearing the mist
that blurs the view.

Hold my hand, my dear

and don't let go.

Walk with me for a while

and let us share precious moments along the way.

The Power of Words

Be aware of your utterances, your way with words,

your speech -

for it can be a double-edged sword.

Slicing through the consciousness,

like salt on a raw, open wound.

Be aware of your utterances, your way with words, your speech -

for it can too, be liberating,

refreshing and empowering -

the feeling of being heard, understood and feeling deeply connected.

Be aware of your utterances, your way with words, your speech -

for it can be the difference between salvation, or perpetually chained to shackles...internally imprisoned.

If only you knew the power, they yield...these words of yours.

Therefore, be aware of your utterances, your way with words, your speech...for they carry much more meaning than mere speech acts.

Life Lesson

You are not someone's saviour. You cannot undo someone's life's journey. That path of awakening is theirs to discover and take.

You can however give them the tools. Although, do remember that ultimately, they are the ones that have to act, you can only invite and encourage them to do so.

Similarly, someone else cannot save/heal *(insert other word of choice)* you. You have to identify, seek, practice and put the work in yourself.

Life Lesson

We use the word death to describe the end of someone's (physical) life but actually, it is not the absolute end of them. Our loved ones are survived *through us.* Manifested in various ways (i.e. prayers/thoughts/actions), that connection surpasses death and elevates it to a much deeper level. It isn't time bound either as it's generally cyclical.

How beautiful, profound, and testament to timeless love is that?

Theme – Journey

The Intrepid Traveller

My free spirit yearns to wander,

to marvel and to exclaim at the world's splendour.

But bound am I by this mundane existence,
preventing me from lands of distance.

So, I set about dreaming of places

of palatial magnificence and beautiful spaces.

Of dense ravines and tranquil scenes,

of sweet nectar bees and lush green trees,

of paradise islands and faraway lands...of turquoise seas and golden sands.

So, I make a pledge; the world I will set off to see,

creating memories and making

those dreams a reality.

If I Should Be No More

If I was to be no more,

and my days on Earth were numbered,

the only regret I would have

are the things I did not do, nor say,

nor the opportunities to be.

And if I was to be no more,

and my days here on Earth were numbered,

I'd have come to the realisation sooner, and taken strides towards the light.

I'd have seen things through more -rather than merely sparing them thoughts.

And if I was to be no more

and my days on Earth were numbered,

I'd have been a little more selfish, and lived for me some more.

I'd have been a little more ruthless, and voiced my inner voice.

Perhaps then, these words would not have come to be -

or events that did not happen,

and regretful orientation too.

Magic Shoes

Not one beautiful shoe but a magical pair,

work that magic and take me there.

Take me to a land unknown,

of sweet blossom trees

and busy honey bees.

Walk me through the promenade,

where towering palm trees sway, and guard.

Magnificent in their tall stature,

protecting all within their capture.

Guide me to the hanging fruits, the sweetness to savour whenever it suits.

Lead the way towards the water,

a gentle balm against the cauter.

Lapping idly against the sandy shore, in rhythmic motions as the eyes explore.

O magical shoes, when we have seen, tasted, felt and spent,

Let us explore yet again

to our heart's content.

Nomad

Like a nomad,

I wander from place to place,

finding temporary shelter where I deem fit.

Like a nomad, I travel far and wide but cannot call a specific place my own.

Like a nomad, I unpack my belongings and acclimatise, with no attachments...lest I spend a little longer and bind myself as a result.

Maybe one day this traveller will find a destination, a state of permanence, a place...to call home.

Journey of Life

Life does not get easier as we travel

through the journey of it.

We just have to become better equipped at dealing with the trials and tribulations that we encounter along the way.

Take comfort in knowing that adversity is temporary and that too, shall pass. Therefore, have courage, faith, and be bold as you encounter and deal with challenges.

Finding Me

I took long walks, walked amongst shadows, tripped on bracken, stumbled and fell.

How I searched, how I sought, how I welcomed opportunities to find the one my heart yearned for.

That special someone to take me out of darkness, to bring me to light and to make me feel whole.

I opened my heart, looked within

and found the one I had been waiting for my entire life.

Me.

Seeking external validation can be a futile task. Look within, and you shall find.

Life Lesson

Learning happens when our thoughts, ideas, actions and behaviour changes by what we have seen, read or experienced. Learning is not static and one does not remain the same or stagnant during the process. Learning is an evolutionary journey

Life Lesson

Enjoy the surprises life brings you, cherish the momentous ones - realise that unpleasant experiences teach us valuable lessons but can also be a blessing.

Spend your time, with those who deserve it - people who make your life special.

Above all, be thankful and appreciate all that you have...life is precious and short!

So, grab opportunities and enjoy.

Life Lesson

Self-confidence is the key to achievement.

Furthermore, it doesn't require money, status and luxuries.

It just requires the strength to say "I can do it. It may not be yet, but I will try. I will persevere, I will not give up".

These self-affirmations will help build the tenacity needed to develop your art as you tentatively take the steps towards mastery.

This journey of life and all that it contains is yours to own, so own it confidently.

Theme - Loss

Deafening Silence

This lull is tiring,
this void, irreplaceable.
This longing, aches...
to hear one word,
to see one smile,
to feel one touch.
Paradoxically, it hurts too -
to think of the impact of such words,
smile,
touch.
Conflictions abound. I don't know how I should feel but
an utterance heard,
a phrase read,
an image seen -
and
I am lost for words.
Lost in time
and space.
Lost in the past
and the beauty of a possible future.

Is it all a dream,

a fantasy,

am I the lost wanderer

or could it become true?

All I know is that I loved being with him, and I yearn to be in his company.

I long to see his eyes sparkle -

his intent gaze.

His gentle mannerisms too.

He made me feel whole.

So now, I live in hope -

For, what else is there,

if there is no hope

Losing You

I lost a part of me when I lost you.

The laughter, the wishes, the colourful dreams...replaced instead with hues of blue.

As though the warmth has disappeared from the raging sun...it rises and sets duty bound but no longer emits intense heat.

As though the light has dimmed from the moon and no longer does it illuminate.

As though a precious gem has lost its sparkle, weathered down - no longer glittering, reflecting the myriad of beauty within.

I lost a part of me when I lost you.

The laughter, the wishes, the colourful dreams...replaced instead with a lifetime of solitude, enveloped in mundane bleakness.

Thoughts of You

In the depths of the nights,

Within the depths of despair,

as my heart bleeds with anguish

with not a tear left to spare.

I reminisce our past, and recall the stories of our lives - days spent in serene bliss,

nights in idyllic hives.

I wish I could reach out to you,

hear the tinkle in your laughter -

look into those smouldering eyes,

burning with desire.

But alas, I awaken from my wishful thoughts,

and push them far away - reassured in the hope...that we will meet again one day.

Forever we will be my love, together once again.

No more heart break, no more yearning...I'll hold out...until then.

A Patchwork of Dreams

I gave you a name,
I gave you an image,
I wove us a story
of a million dreams.
I forget however that
I am not the master weaver,
How little I knew,
that the needle was already broken.
So, I unpick my stitches,
the patchwork swatches -
and heal my sore fingers
until I am ready to sew again.

Tears

I cry for the life we could have made
together - you and me.
I cry for the life we could have had, that just didn't
come to be.
Ordinary things; dining out, taking tea,

flirting outrageously and debating endlessly!
Shopping, staying in, doing 'nothing' -

or when it feels right, doing a lot of something!
But we had to part and go our separate ways, time
passes but the emptiness stays...
It's inconsolable, this grief.
Consumes me from time to time.
I try to move forward but with you, I spent my
prime.
So I cry for the life we could have made,
together you and me.

Life Lesson

Being at one.

When you work through the challenges of cognitive dissonance. When you are at one with your heart and faith, and when you persevere, your actions speak for themselves. The impossible becomes possible, your path is cleared from obstacles and life becomes seamlessly easy.

Please, please, please never underestimate the strength of faith and conviction. It can move mountains and your life can change as a result.

Theme - Hope

Hope

When your heart is breaking into smithereens,
when you are losing sight and sense,
when things descend into chaos and you are fast losing hope.
Hold onto the rope of the almighty,
hold on for stability,
hold on to your inner strength,
hold onto your will and tap into that security.
He sees your helpless tears,
He sees your silent struggles,
He sees your anguished, broken heart and the demons you contend with.
Find solace and comfort in the knowledge that he will never let you down.
Your time will come again my dear,
where you will be whole again.
It's a promise don't you see
that precious assurance guaranteed,
that indeed during hardship,
verily comes ease.

Striving on

I strive on because

light precedes dark - as

day precedes night.

I strive on because

there is calm after a storm - as

stillness ensues after chaos.

I strive on because

the sun rises after it sets -

bringing an assurance of a new tomorrow.

I strive on because I will rise after I fall - time after time after time.

I strive on because I must.

For what else is there? Other than to strive with hope in my heart?

Unpredictability

The future is terrifying,

the unknown leaves me insecure,

the instability petrifying.

but nothing is as scary as remaining where I am...
stagnant, stuck, sick.

Dying a slow,

painful death.

My soul withering away like dust.

So, I will rise against the currents,

the terrifying tides

and ride it out

with hope, with patience

and love.

Foundation

Failure has made me persevere.
Loss has made me stronger.
Weakness has made me bolder.
Despair has given me hope.
Conviction has given me courage.
Tests have taught me patience.
Faith has given me strength.

Life Lesson

If it is meant to be, it will come to pass.

It will happen - somehow, anyhow.

It may be incomprehensible now but believe that it will happen...one day.

Do not lose hope.

Theme - Gratitude

Thank You, Dad

Thank you dad,
for being so strong,
struggling to stay normal
when things were bad.
The meds made you irritable,
made you feel rough.
But you knew should you give up, that things would get tough.
It would shake us and break us
and for us, you wanted more.
So that commanding voice in your head, you tried to ignore.
It wasn't so easy, I know that now -
that voice made perfect sense
amongst everyone's' pretence.
So thank you for making the effort
to lead on as normal,
for coping and making life
okay for us all.
Yes - some times
were tumultuous,
and other times, sad.
But overall, I'm proud to say
that you were my dad.

Life Lesson

Enjoy the surprises life brings you, cherish the momentous ones - realise that unpleasant experiences teach us valuable lessons but can also be a blessing.

Spend your time, with those who deserve it - people who make your life special.

Above all, be thankful and appreciate all that you have...life is precious and short!

So, grab opportunities and enjoy.

Theme – Nature

A Mid Winter's Scene

I look around me
and all I see
is the dreary cold
miserable wind
blowing through the trees.
Once lusciously lined,
now a miserable sight.
The sun obscured out of view, looking sullen -
eclipsed by a blanket of heavy grey clouds.
The westerly wind howling, ripping through the bare
frames of the lonely haggled branches resembling a
rack of ragged ribs.
As night falls, I retreat back indoors and light up a
fire, illuminating the room with its soft glow.
Embracing me with its warmth
and thawing my weary frozen soul...
until I am warm, supple and tender again.

The Lotus Blossom

Emerging from the murky waters,
standing tall and never falters,
With intricate petals within its fold,
the beautiful lotus blossom is a sight to behold.
Wondrously silken, illustriously smooth,
a soft hue in the morning dew.
Standing tall, swaying in its grace,
A perfect stature no matter the place.

Delicate yet resilient.
pure and proud,
Aptly named, so will I,
rise up from the abyss,
with my head held high.

The Oak Tree

A traveller in time and distance and weary from the arduous journey of a thousand painful steps of the past, I found myself facing a mammoth creation.

It struck me how from the blessed humble scattered acorn,

grows the grand oak tree.

Sturdy and strong, trunk-like roots appear dry and dusty above the soil

but run deep, far below the surface of where my feeble feet are placed.

They reach far wide for replenishments and nourishment.

An expansive canopy under which weary souls seek shelter and respite.

A testament of time, and the under-goer of seasons.

Oh, the stories the Oak can tell me of human achievements and fallacies as a witness of space and life.

A vault of hushed whispers and generational secrets as I too share my intimate musings with this silent sturdy confidante. It nods in agreement swaying its wispy branches, it's leaves rustling as if to say *"your secret is safe, speak with conviction".*

I inhale its comforting woody scent, wafting in the breeze as I prepare to sing my tales of woe and betide. Singing in accordance to nature, harmonising in tune as similar and dissimilar as night and day and ever-changing as the seasons and the tides of the sea.

I become at one with nature, a symbiosis of creation - of man and nature.

An Enigmatic Star

Who are you?

Who am I?

What are we supposed to be?

You are an enigma,

a star in the cosmos,

and I, the matter of stardust.

Who knew, across the miles and distance,

You would be a beacon of light.

A miracle of time and space yet with familiarity abound.

Butterfly

I feel a shift taking place,
deep within my soul.
A process just like the metamorphosis of the humble butterfly.
I have crawled and clawed and chomped through life.
Watching and learning and adapting through changes.
Just like the process of metamorphosis of the humble butterfly,
I am undergoing a transition within the safety of my chrysalis.
A shift is most definitely taking place like the pupa of a butterfly.
The change is terrifying and exciting in equal measures.
Do I stay cocooned within safety, or dare to make that leap into the unknown?
Yes, the familiar and the unknown
are both daunting, each with a chain reaction that may follow.
But I feel that like the final process of metamorphosis, the time has come for me to emerge from a humble caterpillar to a fluttering butterfly.

The Lonely Canary

Oh, how the canary from afar, looks carefree and well looked after.

frolics and flutters and chirps loudly,

weaned, watered, ruffled and cleaned.

Look a little closer and it's apparent to see the wings are clipped, ever so slightly.

The cage, the wired cage, was home for a while.

But now, the baby canary has grown -

It wants to live, forge a life of its own.

But alas, those years spent in solitary confinement

has rendered it incapable through doubt and torment.

"It's not so bad" the canary consoles "my needs are met and I have no woes.

I can see the world - view it from within.

I can watch without a tumble, whilst others' trip and stumble".

But reality strikes..."It's terribly bleak"

“This life is empty and I am weak!

This cage I have found myself herein, from which, I accept I will never escape”.

The lonely caged canary, who sings so sweetly

of life, of losses and of melancholy,

bides its time with thoughts sublime.

The Glorious Star – The Sun

Each traversing in its orbit, the Earth and the moon, are engaged in circumnavigation.

Ordained and compelled by divine order, a system decreed by a gravitational force.

Hailed as a deity, revered and worshipped too, it is none other than the powerful sun.

A glorious star; and many would agree that it is a tangible presence of Allah's creation and mercy.

Withstanding reverence from past civilisations - the Aztecs, Egyptians, and the Persian Pagans by

erecting monuments of great stature for the pleasure of tilling and harvesting the sun's treasure.

A raging sphere of hot mass; it nourishes, strengthens and sustains life. Permeating through to the evolution on Earth, from seedlings to trees - and mankind too. It is a paradox between existence and extinction.

Admire from afar, lest the intense, dazzling flares decimate.

Witness it rising from the East with the promise of a breaking dawn. Embrace the hazy setting in the

West, and the array of dusky hues painting the skies pink and blue.

More than just a central star to the solar system, it is a voice of conviction that whispers;

"Till the end of time,

till you breathe your last,

till you are no more, and you've turn to dust.

Have belief in what you see yonder,

for in it are signs for those who ponder.

As the Almighty creator in his last scripture; asserts,

"Then which of the favours of your Lord will you deny?"

(Inspiration: Quran 36:40 and 55:13)

Moon Power

Such is the power of the moon that it causes stirs in emotions of people and brings forth changes in nature.

It shines by its own merit, its illuminating crown lighting up the paths of all those who seek it.

It does not compete for light and magnificence, for it is majestic by design.

It reigns the night skies, with even the seas moving rhythmically to its splendour.

So too, be that force whose humble presence lights and illuminates those around you.

Moon

Thank you for being steadfast and constant.

Your unwavering commitment to appear cyclically has seen many changes in my life.

I have fallen, infallible as I am but

I muster the will to get up. Gathering strength from all that enables me growth.

You, my beautiful moon ground me, you fill me with awe, you are a silent, powerful force...and you grace your immense presence silently but with bold conviction. Your words being "I see you, I am here...and change is inevitable (as night befalls day)" which you must embrace.

The celestial body, the moon - a regular tangible presence throughout the events of life.

The constant, come what may.

The Moon

O beautiful moon, majestic moon,

taking your place in the night sky. Your cyclical presence;

waxing, waning, new and full - illuminates the world with your luminescence.

O majestic moon, enveloping the hope of many as you carry forward, being the constant, come what may.

O majestic moon; how in your presence, I have conversed, hoped, wished and prayed.

Through the seasons and the tide,

you remain the reliable source

of light, energy and majestic splendour.

O what an awe inspiring and breath-taking blessing you truly are!

The Celestial Crown

The powerful force that is the radiance of the moon
draws me in. Thus, I find myself

gravitating

orientating

inclining

towards the magnet it is.

It is sheer amazing how the fascination continues and
the anticipation keeps me coming back

month

after month

after month.

I do not tire at this magnificent sight for I am like a
child on the journey of discovery

wanting to find

wanting to learn

wanting to behold.

I gaze up enthralled and enraptured at the luminous
night sky. Adorned with an arrangement of sparkling
gems that

glitter

and glow

and complement

the celestial crown...the moon.

Nature's Awakening

I stir from a languid state.

Stirring somewhere between consciousness and slumber by a distant sound.

As it continues, I begin to awaken from the sweet singing of the morning thrush.

The melodious tone lulling me gently,

easing me out of sleep.

I pay heed to the sweet songs of glory, a beautiful reminder that dawn has begun.

The vast sky, an adornment of resplendent colours is a breath taking one.

It is a welcome, enveloped in an array of pink hues, with undertones of lilac contrasted with lustrous golds.

I take in the beauty of nature and the magnificence that it bestows -the gift of another day.

I stand there

in awe

in humility

and in gratitude

of all that I behold.

Prey

I bought my owner another gift today, twice in one day - oh she must be proud!

It was a thrilling game, an exhilarating chase in which I teased and lured

and waited and preyed!

Our battlefield was vast, it scurried here and there, back and forth to every nook and cranny.

Darting between the cast iron pipes, the slabs of concrete, and the pieces of pottery.

Yes, the playground was vast - entwined with brambles, scraggly shrubs and uninvited weeds.

With grass that rustled in the northerly wind, strong and weathered, representing reeds.

This ragged terrain was perfect for me, my coat blended well and I was well tended.

Oh, the fun, the joy, the exuberant moment

as I pounced upon that pesky creature!

Within a blink of an eye, I was there, swooping and scooping its trembling body. I tightened my grip around its scrawny neck. Laying still, it played dead -

no whimpering, no squeaking, no twitchy whiskers. The end was nigh, its breathing shallowed. Its life ebbing out, exhausted and laboured.

The triumph was mine - this game of chase. Such is life - this survival of place!

We fight for the hierarchy - to earn our keep.

Today I win - for now, I retreat - returning home with a treat!

Chasing Rainbows

A heady combination,

of rain and shine -

the elusive rainbow, oh what a sight - the fascination!

I marvel at its grand stature, the everlasting width,
from breadth to depth.

Enthralled, I make a little wish under its colourful
embrace, as it transforms the bleak land into a
magical place.

Within its precious splendour, I am enveloped, I
savour the moment and enjoy the encounter -
knowing full well what to expect a little later.

Chasing rainbows; leprechauns and gold – I have
learnt is a futile pursuit.

How I have waited and pleaded for the hues to stay,
but this works against nature...which I cannot refute.

Experiences have taught me to appreciate this
treasure, to bask in this relationship between man
and nature, to revel in awe and admiration and
pleasure...but painful as it is, eventually to let go.

An Islamic Garden.

Whitewashed walls, a water-feature, colourful
geometry and
the simplicity of nature.
Typical features found
in an Islamic garden -
a centre created
for rest and reflection.
The harmony, serenity as well as the purity -
the Islamic garden is about beauty and tranquillity.
"Gardens underneath which rivers flow" is realised in
an Islamic garden,

So enjoy the flora and the fauna,
around a centre-piece.
Enjoy the sounds of the gentle waves - as you reflect
and admire.

Tweets of The Early Morning Thrush

I awake gently to the sweet sounds of the morning
thrush.
The rhapsodies reverberating through my ears, my
mind and
reaching my soul.
The soulful tone reassuring me
that beauty is present, as nature intended.
I am reminded of you,
naturally intriguing, gentle yet powerful.
Reminds me of your sweet words and your
thoughtful gestures.
I need not worry, I need not be afraid.
I will allow that beautiful melody to
soothe and salve as I pave my way.

Taking Flight

I flew away
to forge a new tomorrow,
from the bleakness of my routine,
from the mundaneness of the sorrow.

I embarked on an exciting journey
of self-satisfaction
and
discovery.

I saw and I did,
and I tasted and I slid...
I rushed and I ran -
my journey had just began!

But after the running, and after
the trying,
my heart was unfulfilled
and my soul, crying.

I was tired of playing the game -
decided to fly back,
I turned towards you
my head bowed in shame.

But your promise to every believer -
you kept my almighty lord -
you didn't just turn and wait,
You walked, my creator.

I have had the epiphany,
now seen the beautiful light.
My restless heart is now at peace,
beating to a serene symphony.

Thank you my lord for shining the light, that bought this wayfarer back.
Thank you for illuminating the path, making it so wondrous and bright.

Bird Singing in the Dead of Night

I hear the melodious songs
of the birds of the night.
Singing ever so sweetly with all their might.
Their ranges differ, not a note out of place, these
creatures transport me to another realm and space.
No worries, no stress, but calm and peace - with the
birds who are perched high up in the trees.
A comfort indeed which serves as a reminder that
the creator neglects me not, and is kinder..
To send me companions in the dead of night; who
with their sweet tones,
assures me that things will be alright.
With the gentle breeze rustling through the curtains,
and the songs becoming more faint, one thing of
which I am becoming certain...
I am being lulled back to sleep by the melodious
songs of the birds of the night.

Life Lesson

Own your journey of lessons, trials and tribulations, for they will ultimately help you grow. Use your struggles as a catalyst for growth and prosperity.

Theme - Wound

Your Words

Your words cut deep.

The blades of your tongue piercing through my skin

and

penetrating into my heart, slashing the chambers within.

The etched words, the internal wounds bleed no longer

for they have

become

scars.

Lot

You may have had my time

You may have expended my energy

You may have occupied my space

You may have spent my money

You may have consumed my food

and ravished my body.

But you will *never* have the most inner, the most sacred part of me...

my soul, and what lies within.

Try as you may, my soul you cannot crush.

So, enjoy the relish of what you see as your worldly gain, for it is all transient.

You will never have within your grasp this everlasting, eternal, insurmountable, strong spirit of mine

and that

is

my gain.

The Power of Words

Be aware of your utterances, your way with words,

your speech -

for it can be a

double-edged sword.

Slicing through the consciousness,

like salt on a raw, open wound.

Be aware of your utterances, your way with words,
your speech -

for it can too, be liberating,

refreshing and empowering -

the feeling of being heard, understood and feeling
deeply connected.

Be aware of your utterances, your way with words,
your speech -

for it can be the difference between salvation, or
perpetually chained to shackles...internally
imprisoned.

If only you knew the power, they yield...these words
of yours.

Therefore, be aware of your utterances, your way
with words, your speech...for they carry much more
meaning than mere speech acts.

Life Lesson:

Tend to your wounds and heal
so that you do not bleed on those
who did not cut you

Theme - Self-worth

Labels

You are not your labels.

You are much more than that.

Allow your heart to guide you to the person that you are (supposed to be).

Let your purity speak, let it show them

who you truly are.

Live life on your terms, not by who they think you are or who they think you ought to be.

You are not your labels.

You are not other peoples' expectations, nor their projections.

You are uniquely you and therein lies your beauty.

You

Build a relationship with yourself first.

Get to know you;

your thoughts

your feelings

your emotions

your triggers

your breaths

your quirks

your dark side too.

Everyone and everything else are secondary.

You cannot expect to receive from others if you do not receive yourself.

You cannot be expected to be understood if you do not understand yourself.

You cannot pour into the cup of others if your own cup is empty.

Get to know you.

You

matter.

Do Not Weep for Me

Do not weep for me my dear, for my tears have crystallised into rare gems and no longer pool into seas of tears.

Do not despair for me my dear, for I am now an anchor of hope, who firmly has her sturdy, hardy roots spread out for stability.

Do not fear for my loss, for I am not alone. I have an armour of love from within and of those around me.

Overall, do not be afraid for me.

I am bold, I am courageous and I am a warrior.

I fight my own battles - silent or otherwise.

Her Eyes

Her haunting eyes locked with mine
and I could see the anguish.
The silent rejections,
the broken promises,
the hushed voice.
Her intense eyes locked with mine
and I could see steely determination.
A burning passion,
A staunch conviction
A propelled drive.
Her bright eyes locked with mine
and I could see
a survivor.
A woman on a mission,
driven
ambitious
committed.

Cheap Perfume

My cheap perfume does not reflect my self-worth
nor does it reflect my self-value.

So, do not use it as a measure of me.

My cheap perfume reflects my confidence.

It reflects my will to step out boldly, in whatever I am wearing.

Unafraid, proud, unfiltered and unmasked.

I do not care to impress with expensive scents, to
mask an inner stench with selected fragrances.

I am not one for keeping up a false pretence, of
keeping up appearances.

My cheap perfume is perfectly placed, worn with
pride and timely.

It is not a reflection of my self-worth and value.

Skin Deep

The mind is young,
the eyes can still see.
But the body is failing,
feels as old as can be.
It feels weathered and
bothered and tattered too.
Add wrinkles, lines and 'hide'
that has leathered!
And there'll be a cocktail
of ingredients in the mix,
to feel insecure to
a time before.
But let me give you some pearls and gems of
wisdom,
that perhaps this *filtered* era lacks.
Beauty is skin deep -
and lies with the beholder.
Never mind if with time I get older.
I shall resort to life as I please,
perhaps only then, judgements will cease!

Live In The Now

Live in the moment,
For this is life, this is what matters and what is important.
So channel your energy and focus on now, for this moment right now is life.
Don't worry about what has or hasn't happened and may/may not come to be.
Don't be sad at what was, what isn't and what could have been,
for this moment right now is life.
Smile at the past and you will see that they were keepsake tokens, to be cherished.
Be true to the job at hand and focus.
Nurture, cherish and love wholeheartedly by living in the now.
For this moment right now is life.

Reflection

If you want to meet someone who will change your life,

look in the mirror.

Look at that person through a different set of lenses.

One of compassion

One of kindness

One of mercy

and forgiveness.

One of encouragement

One of bravery

One of determination

and success.

You are amazing through the eyes of others. See yourself through those very lenses too.

Life Lesson

Perception

When you start cultivating the seeds of self-worth,

You will see yourself in a new light with a new set of lenses.

Furthermore, you will have a new sense of energy invigoration and your network will inadvertently change too, reflecting that.

Thus, it will be difficult to be around people who don't share or radiate the energy you exude.

You will orientate towards people who do.

This is growth.

Theme – Growth

Self-Growth

Self-growth occurs with a reflection, spark, a recognition of wanting more for yourself - that you deserve more. This leads to a desire to grow. Once you have that recognition, you set yourself boundaries, healthy ones (of course).

These changes are cataclysmic and they shift your locus of perception. At this point, you associate with those who encourage your growth and you no longer have the energy to be around those who do not see your worth. If it is not possible to remove them from your life then you realise that their perception, views and opinions do not hold any weight in relation to you.

That is when growth takes place.

Painful Process

It is painful that I didn't recognise my worth -

that I sought it in the validation of others.

It is painful now knowing that I led life
compromising my own happiness, for the fulfilment
of others.

It is painful knowing that I just settled -

that I did not give me my all.

It is painful knowing that I poured into the cup of
others

whilst mine was dry, beseeching to be filled.

Coming to this realisation too, is painful.

But what is growth if not being able to recognise and
reconcile,

if not to repair and remedy?

What is growth if not to challenge ill-gotten gains?

What is growth if not being able to take confident
strides ahead whilst acknowledging past stumbles?

Growth is painful

but it is well worth

the pain.

Burden Free

New spring in my step, my head held high.

I stare intently, a woman on a mission.

I breathe in the air and it fills my chest. I feel relieved - no burden,

worries, no fear.

It feels good to breathe, not heave nor sigh.

No more looking back, no more downcast -

no more weights to crush my soul.

I feel light as a feather, weightless and giddy with freedom.

With the anticipation of surprises, the pleasures and experiences new.

I view the world as if for the first time.

Taking in the smells, the sights, the wonderful delights,

that dazzle and bedazzle

and light up bright

my bleak, dull existence

that was until now.

I am now free,

not bound from within.

I can go as I please

without a care.

Continuity

Soldiering on when
I just want to collapse...
now, that is my struggle.
Remaining upbeat when I feel downtrodden...
now, that is my struggle.
Fulfilling my duties
when feeling let-down by...
now, that is my struggle.
Smiling through a wall of tears...
now, that is my struggle.
Looking forward despite the pain
of yesterday...
now, that is my struggle.
Reaching out despite
my pain and anguish...
now, that is my struggle.
My struggle is real, raw, and ravenous...
but I will strive on.

I Am Enough

I love myself, as I am.

I accept myself in my entirety - my flaws, my imperfections, my selfless/selfishness.

I realise I am not infallible - I am indeed fallible. The beauty being able to get up after I fall.

I am human and I am life, I am living, and it's enough.

I see beauty, in the creation of this beautiful planet, and in the creativity of humans, nature and more.

I appreciate the gifts I receive wanted and otherwise and they teach me this - that I am enough.

I have always been enough and will continue to be.

Healing

Dear self, I will heal

and rebuild and become whole once more.

Dear dreams, I will deconstruct the shattered ones, and build new ones.

Dear memories, I will focus on the beautiful and make more memorable ones.

Dear life, I appreciate you, I love you and I will strive on.

Comparisons

Too often, one's success is measured against another's ruler. Especially in this time of a more globalised, connected world and online social media presence. Everyday there are newsfeeds and comparisons abound.

Do remember however, beneath the face value of what you see, there was a journey undertaken and it may have been arduous.

Be inspired by what you see of course but recognise that your life cannot be compared to another. This is *your* life, and it is unique to you.

You are the blueprint of it and for it.

It is not a one-size-fits-all criteria.

You are the journey and the footprints are unique to you.

Striving On

I strive on because

light precedes dark - as

day precedes night.

I strive on because

there is calm after a storm - as

stillness ensues after chaos.

I strive on because

the sun rises after it sets -

bringing an assurance of a new tomorrow.

I strive on because I will rise after I fall - time after time after time.

I strive on because I must.

For what else is there? Other than to strive with hope in my heart?

I Am Enough

I love myself, as I am.

I accept myself in my entirety - my flaws, my imperfections, my selfless/selfishness.

I realise I am not infallible - or I am.

I am human and I am life, I am living, and it's enough.

I see beauty, in the creation of this beautiful planet, and in the creativity of humans, nature and more.

I appreciate the gifts I receive wanted and otherwise and they teach me this - that I am enough.

I have always been enough and will continue to be.

Gains and Wins

Failure has made me persevere.
Loss has made me stronger.
Weakness has made me bolder.
Despair has given me hope.
Conviction has given me courage.
Tests have taught me patience.
Faith has given me strength.

Strength

Have a mind that is impenetrable,

a desire driven by goals.

Have a fire that is inextinguishable,

raging with passion inside.

Have a heart full of conviction and belief in your heart.

Be the best form that you can be

of yourself, for yourself -

thrive and achieve.

Creature of Habit

O creature of habit,

stop seeking to please others.

O creature of habit,

stop seeking to build a home

in someone else's heart.

Seek a home in your *own* heart,

for in that lies contentment and fulfilment that does not seek to be filled by worthless pursuits.

O creature of habit,

change your habit.

Make your heart a place of peace, security,

comfort and serenity

O creature of habit,

come

back

home.

Life Lesson

Your own challenges, trials, goals and milestones cannot be compared to another's. Similarly, nor can your achievements.

This journey of life and all that it contains is yours to own, so own it.

Worry not much about failing, for it is also part of life. Failing multiple times will make your win that much sweeter.

Glossary

Circumnavigation – the action of completely going around something – to circumnavigate.

Dua - the act of supplication, meaning to 'call out' in Arabic

Quran – the holy, sacred book in Islam

He – 'He' is referred to as God (according to the Islamic faith)

www.ingramcontent.com/pod-product-compliance
Lightning Source LLC
Chambersburg PA
CBHW022158160726
48282CB00024B/236
* 9 7 8 9 3 9 1 5 1 9 1 6 2 *